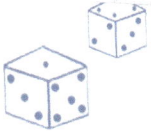

# SPEECHIE SQUEEZE!

By Maya Greer, M.Ed., M.S., CF-SLP
Illustrated by QBN Studios

To every child who has ever felt nervous about finding their voice— this is for you.

And to my family, friends, and the little ones who inspire me every day— thank you for believing in me, cheering me on, and reminding me why I do what I do.

With all my heart, Maya

## This book belongs to:

_____

Official Member of the Speechie Squeeze Squad!
Let the games, giggles, and growing begin!

Knock, knock!

"It's the Speech Therapist!" says the teacher. "She's here to help students work on their speech sounds!"

"For the next 30 minutes, we'll have a little fun while learning how to make our speech sounds better!" says the speech therapist.

"What are speech sounds?" Olivia asks. "Great question! Let me explain! Speech sounds are the little sounds we make when we talk. Like the /b/ in bat or the /s/ in sock.

Aa Bb Cc Dd Ee Ff Gg Hh Ii Jj Kk Ll Mm
Nn Oo Pp Qq Rr Ss Tt Uu Vv Ww Xx Yy Zz

"We use them to make words and talk to each other! Shhh, did you know words can be magical when we say them just right?" whispers the speech therapist.

"Sometimes, kids say 'tat' instead of 'cat.' That's when I bring them to my room to help them fix those silly sounds!"

/tat/ for /cat/

"Alright, Michelle and Mason, it's time to get started!
Ready? Let's goooooo! Off to my room we go!"

The speech therapist and children sing:

"We're walking, walking down the hallway... Lalala, like a dancing penguin! "We're walking, walking down the hallway... Lalala- like a dancing penguin!"

"We're here! Time to get to work! Let's work on your /p/ sounds, Mason. Michelle, we're going to practice your /l/ sounds!" says the speech therapist.

"I'm nervous about practicing my /l/ sounds," Michelle says.

"It's okay, don't be nervous! Practice helps us get better! And guess what? We have a fun game to make it even more exciting!" replies the speech therapist.

"Let's feed the monster! You'll say the word five times and then feed it to the monster! Yum! The monster loves to eat!"

"Let's go, Mason! Say 'pig' five times!"

"Pig, pig, pig, pig, pig!" says Mason.

"Now, Michelle, say 'love' five times. Remember, your tongue goes at the top, behind your teeth!" says the speech therapist.

Michelle says, "L-l-love..."

Michelle tries, but her voice wobbles.

It doesn't sound quite right.

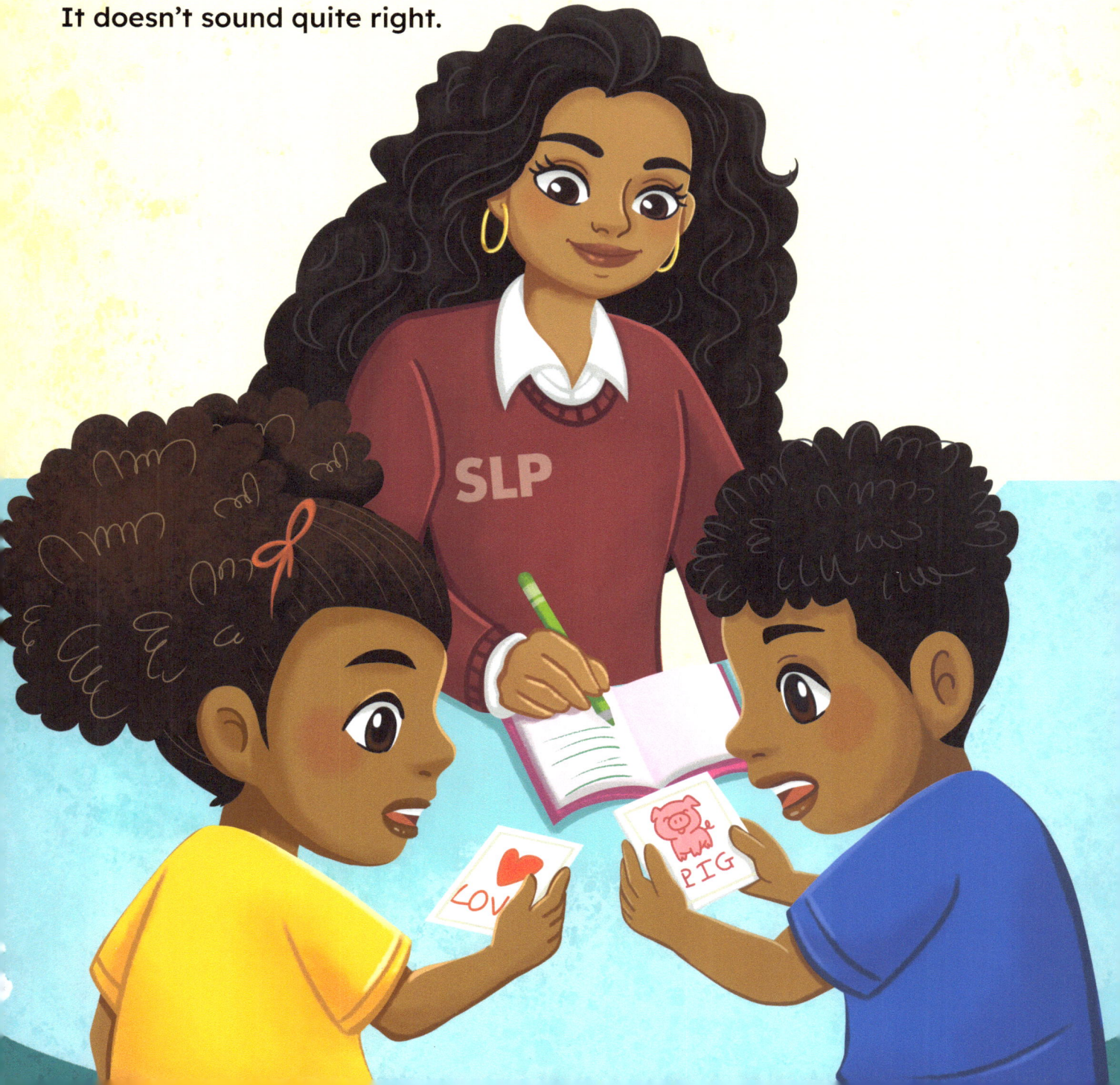

Michelle sadly says, "I can't do it."

"Oh no, Michelle! It's okay! Words can be tricky sometimes. Let's be detectives and figure it out together! Let's try again, nice and slow. Ready? Let's take a deep breath like you're smelling flowers..." says the speech therapist.

"Now say it with me, one... two... three..."

"Whoo hoo! That was fantastic Michelle!" shouts Mason.

The speech therapist says, "Great job, everyone! You're doing awesome!"

"Let's play the Speech Dice Game next! Roll the dice, say the word with the right sound and move your game piece forward! Will the dice give you the magical sound you need to win? Roll and find out!"

"Roll the dice! Michelle, you go first!"

Michelle says "Okay, here I go!"

Say 'leaf' three times and move your piece." explains the speech therapist. Mason says, "Now it's my turn!"

"That's right, Mason!" says the speech therapist.

He rolls his dice and it lands on five!

"Say 'pie' five times and move your piece!" Great job practicing your sounds! You both are really getting the hang of it!"

PIE

END

The speech therapist says, "Let's make a sound like a monster for saying our sounds correctly!"

# GRHHHHHHH!!!

"That was so much fun! You both worked really hard today! Before you go back to class, choose a gift from the mystery box!"

"We're back! You each did an amazing job in speech today!"

Aa Bb Cc Dd Ee F.
Nn Oo Pp Qq Rr Ss

Olivia shouts, "I want to go to speech!"

Issac says, "Take me!"

Teacher says, "Alright, class..."

Gg Hh Ii Jj Kk Ll Mm
Uu Vv Ww Xx Yy Zz

The speech therapist says, "Great job today! Keep practicing, I'll see you next time for more fun!"

# About the author:

Maya N. Greer is a newly graduated speech-language pathologist who was born and raised in Jackson, Mississippi. She has always had a passion for working with children and dreamed of one day bringing her work to life through a children's book.

*Speechie Squeeze!* is Maya's very first book—an idea that started in her heart and grew from her real-life experiences helping kids find their voice. She hopes this story makes every child feel seen, supported, and proud of their progress.

When she's not working with children or writing, Maya enjoys traveling, spending time with the ones she loves, and dreaming up new ways to grow as an entrepreneur. She believes in leading with purpose, joy, and a whole lot of heart.